Published by Darf Children's Books
An imprint of Darf Publishers Ltd
277 West End Lane
West Hampstead
London
NW6 1QS

Nour's Escape
By Abir Ali,
Illustrated by Gulnar Hajo

First Published in Arabic by Bright Fingers Publishing House, Damascus - Syria 2015
Originally published as نور تهرب من القصة (Noor tahrub min al qasa)

Translated by Ruth Ahmedzai Kemp
Edited by Sherif Dhaimish

© 2015 Storyline Abir Ali, Illustrations Gulnar Hajo

The moral right of the author has been asserted

All rights reserved

This book is sold subject to the condition that it shall not, by way of trade or otherwise,
be lent, resold, hired out, or otherwise circulated without the publisher's prior consent
in any form of binding or cover other than that in which it is published and without a similar condition, including
this condition, being imposed on the subsequent purchaser.

A catalogue record of this book is available from the British Library.

Printed and bound in Turkey by Elma Basim

ISBN-13: 978-1-85077-328-3

www.darfpublishers.co.uk

Nour's Escape

Abir Ali
Illustrated by Gulnar Hajo

Adil was an ordinary boy. He's probably playing quietly in his room right now. But one day something happened to him that wasn't ordinary at all.
It was nothing short of magical!

His mum said that every morning before he could go outside and play, he must read a book.
At first, he wished a heavy rainstorm would come and wash away all his books.
He found it hard to read a whole book at once.

But day by day he found it more enjoyable.
Until one day he realised that he loved reading and he loved his books.

What Adil didn't realise was that when we read with love, something magical happens.

One day, Adil picked up a story about Nour.
She was a little girl who didn't have a family
or a home. She lived on a street somewhere
far away and long ago.

Nour's clothes and hair were always dirty.
When night fell, Nour had to sleep on the pavement.
Hardly anyone helped her, and her face was always
tired and sad.

Adil read the story aloud, so that his mum could
hear him from the other room.

But Adil didn't know that inside each book there
is a whole world that is asleep until a reader
wakes it up... When Adil began to read, Nour
woke up. So did the street and the passers-by...

Life seeped into the little book,
but sadly it wasn't a very nice life for Nour.

Adil had got to the line that said, "The lady refused to help Nour…" when the phone rang. He didn't finish the sentence. He ran to answer the phone.

But he didn't realise that when we stop reading halfway through a line, the character in the book stays awake while the story goes back to sleep. Did you know that?

For the first time in her life, Nour was left wide awake while her story was asleep. Everything in her story stopped.

The boy who was jumping on the pavement stopped in mid-air. The man in the window of the house opposite stopped mid-sneeze. He looked funny like that. But why had it happened?

Nour was confused. She rubbed her eyes three times. She pinched her arm and her cheek to see if she was dreaming… She even tried banging her head against the street lamp next to her.

Nour thought she must be dreaming. Soon she would wake up and everything would go back to normal.

But that didn't happen.

She walked around, but everywhere she looked she was the only person or thing that moved.

But then something even stranger happened. She looked up and gasped in shock.
The sky was green! There were two suns and a white cloud with three enormous arms.

Nour was so afraid, she began to cry.

She didn't realise that she was looking out of her story and into Adil's bedroom, which had two lights and a big white fan on the ceiling.

Nour quickly ran to hide in the bakery nearby.
The smell of bread hadn't completely gone to sleep.
Nour breathed in the delicious smell and
remembered that she was starving!

Then she heard a faint voice.
"Go on, take some," it said. "There's no one here
to notice! You are poor, after all. Here's your chance.
Fill your pockets with bread, money and sweets!"

Nour shuddered. But her stomach rumbled.

She stretched out her hand to take some bread,
but then she didn't dare.

She rushed out of the bakery.

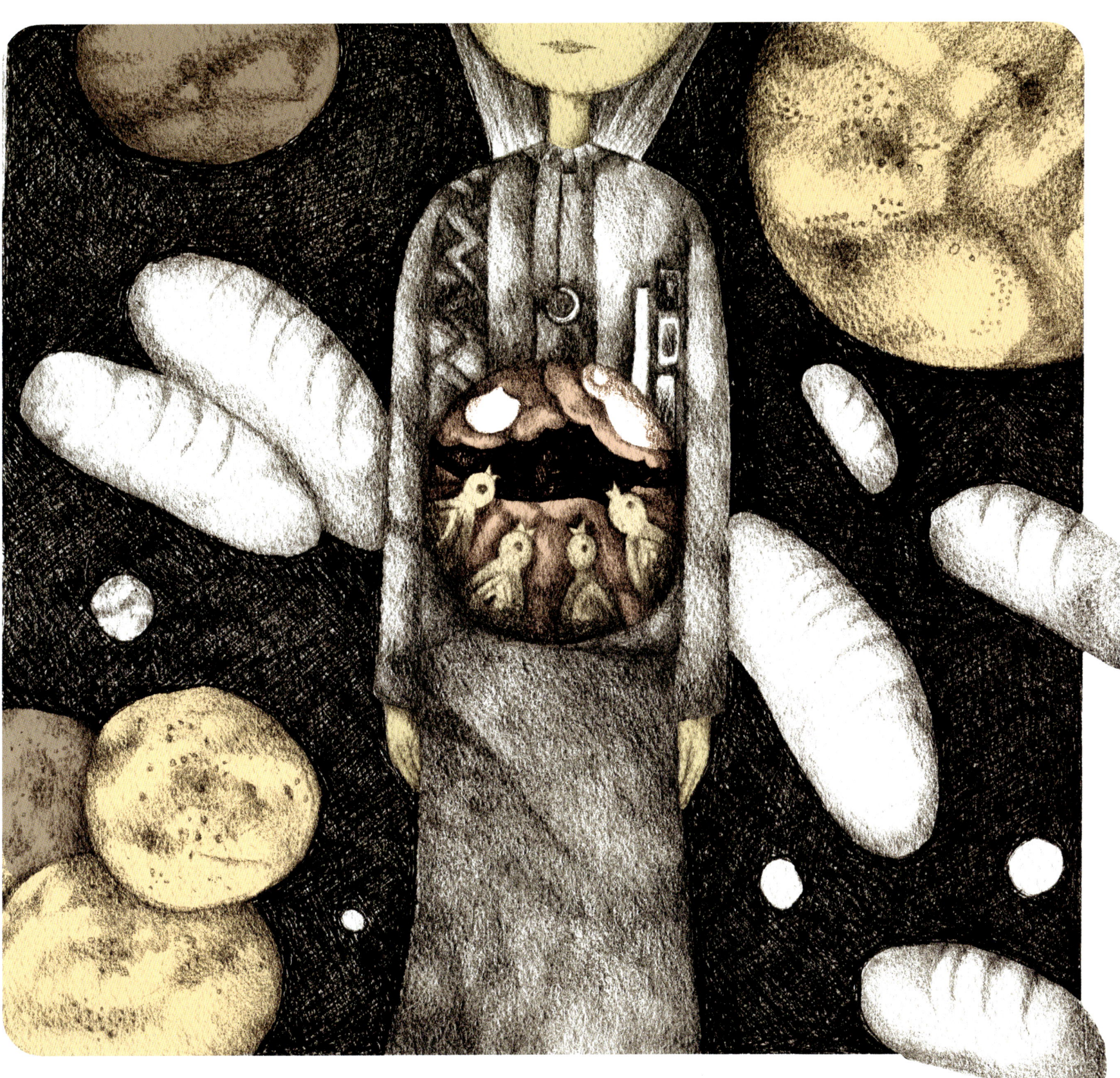

"You coward!" came the voice again.
"You're always scared. That's why your life is so horrid. Look around you! Everyone else is happy. They've got nice clothes to wear, delicious food to eat, friends. You don't have anything! You're a scaredy-cat who can't even steal a loaf of bread!"

Nour felt a rush of anger. Tears came to her eyes and her head filled with fire.

"Who are you?" Nour shouted. "Where are you? Why don't you come out and show your face?"

But she couldn't see anyone.

She just heard the voice again. "I'm here with you. I'll always be here, you scaredy-cat."

Nour didn't know what to say.

"Why don't I have a nice life too?" she asked herself. "I want to be happy!"

The only answer came from the annoying voice.

"Your story is sad," said the voice, "but you can't get away from it. You sleep with it when it sleeps, and it always wakes up before you.

There's no escape!"

The words rang in Nour's head like a giant golden bell!

"Escape?" Nour thought.
"What if I could actually escape?"

She desperately wanted to, but can characters run away from their own stories?

Nour didn't know the answer.
And anyway, she didn't dare to try and find out.

"Didn't I say you were a coward?" said the voice.

Before Nour could think any more about escaping, Adil came back and carried on reading.

The story woke up again and Nour couldn't get away from what was written down.

But an idea had been planted in her heart.
She suddenly had a burning desire to live a new life, a different one.

Nour longed for Adil to stop reading again.

Just as Nour had wished, Adil's mum called him and he ran out of the room, leaving Nour wide awake in her story.

This time Nour took a deep breath.

She closed her eyes and put her hands over her ears, so she wouldn't hear the horrible voice.

She ran as fast as she could...
She ran and ran and didn't stop...
And she did it!

Nour managed to escape from her story.

But where was she now? It was all so strange ...

Poor Nour didn't realise she had turned from a character in a story into an idea floating in space. And ideas can't be touched or seen.

Nour looked down but she couldn't see herself. She couldn't feel her hands or her feet.

She wanted to cry, but she didn't have any eyes. She wanted to shout, but she didn't have a mouth or a tongue to make a sound.

She thought about going back, but she didn't know how to get there. It was like she was flying!

أَصْرُخ
أَعُودُ
أَبْكِي
أَطِيرُ
أَطِيرُ
أَصْرُخ

Then, out of nowhere, Nour heard the annoying voice again. It had followed her!

"So, you really did escape!" said the voice in surprise. "But what are you going to do now?"

Nour felt lost and afraid. She didn't have a body. No one could hear her or see her.

She felt like she was falling…

Down and down she fell, until she landed on Adil's bedroom rug. No one knew she was there, of course.

The voice let out a loud, menacing laugh.
It echoed like the sound of thunder.
"Scaredy-cat, scaredy-cat!"

"I'm not a scaredy-cat," Nour thought.
"I managed to escape from my own story!"

As soon as she thought that, she started to feel a bit lighter. She started to hover a few centimetres above the floor.

She looked down in amazement.

She realised that when the voice laughed at her, she was weighed down by fear and sadness. As soon as she threw off those feelings, she felt lighter and braver.

She began to fly up and up!

Nour laughed from deep inside.
Her laughter chased away all the fear.
She was flying and she was happy.

The higher she rose, the further behind
she left the voice.

"Please, Nour! Don't leave me here," it called
from down on the floor. "I was mean to you.
Please forgive me and let's be friends again!"

Nour thought for a moment. The voice had been
mean to her, but Nour didn't want to be unkind.
She decided to give the voice one more chance.

She let the voice come with her.

Being kind and forgiving can make you feel lighter.

No sooner had she forgiven the voice than she floated up like a balloon, high into the sky.

She was happy and carefree.

But she still didn't have a body you could see or a story you could read. She was just an idea floating in the sky.

Nour wanted to find a new story to live in: one that was nicer and more comfortable, one where she had a family and friends. And maybe a new name.

She can't write a story for herself, but she can visit the imagination of anyone who lets her in.

Perhaps you could write Nour a new story and help her find the happy life she's been looking for?